# Transcripts for Daily Living

## Relationship Edition

Gaylyn,
Blessings over your journey
as you allow God to play His
song through you!

In Gratitude,
Leah Gonzales

By Leah Gonzales

*Transcripts for Daily Living, Relationship Edition*
*Copyright © 2014 by Leah Gonzales*
*Printed in the United States of America*

*ISBN: 978-0-9892427-1-4*

*Published by Leah Gonzales*
*Pearland, TX*

*All Scripture quotations are taken from the Amplified (AMP), King James Version (KJV) and New International Version (NIV) of the Bible.*

*For additional copies of Transcripts for Daily Living contact Leah Gonzales at leahg06@sbcglobal.net.*

# Contents

# *Introduction*

Transcripts for Daily Living, Relationship Edition, is a 30-day devotional geared toward promoting intentionality when interacting with those around us. We were designed through relationship and for relationship. Our life on this earth was only made possible as a result of a relationship. Hence, even if it was the product of a bad relationship or a brief relationship, even still, it was definitely the result of a relationship.

As we nurture the horizontal connections with one another, it gives us a little taste of what we can expect to receive from the vertical connection with our Heavenly Father. Nevertheless, the vertical connection needs to be deep and abiding if we truly want to create lasting and meaningful horizontal connections. As most everything fades away, relationships are the only things that are transferrable to our eternal resting place. The connections we make through relationships are everlasting because they are contained in our hearts which serve as indestructible eternal vessels that enable them to make the journey.

Throughout the day we are faced with numerous opportunities to have an extraordinary impact not only on existing relationships but on every person whose path with which we intersect. From a Godly perspective, every encounter is divine and extremely purposeful. May we never see another encounter from a humanistic perspective but see it as a divine appointment which will yield an eternal impact.

# Dedication

I dedicate this book to my family who first recognized my writing abilities in homemade greeting cards I sent to them on special occasions. They encouraged me to continue to pursue inspirational writing. As a result of them believing in my writing abilities, it provided the affirmation I needed to yield to God when He called me to start a blog and to put my daily devotionals in book format.

Special thanks to my husband, Juan Gonzales, who served as the editor and design manager. He played an integral role in making the dream of publishing a book become reality.

# DAY 1

# A Commodity That Money Can't Buy

*You show that you are a letter from Christ, the result of our ministry, written not with ink but with the Spirit of the living God, not on tablets of stone but on tablets of human hearts.*

*– 2 Corinthians 3:3 (NIV)*

**W**hat do you have that money can't buy? As I entered a difficult season in life I had to explore this very question. Previous to this difficult season, I was by no means rich according to the world's standards. Nevertheless, by the frugal way I managed my finances I typically always had something extra to give. During the difficult season, despite my frugal lifestyle, I didn't have any extra money to spare.

As we know, life goes on regardless of our financial difficulties. There are still pleas from every organization in need of financial assistance. There are still special occasions amongst family and friends where gift exchange is prevalent. At the beginning of the difficult season, I was saddened and hung my head in embarrassment because I had nothing tangible to give.

With the absence of material gifts, it prompted me to look within to discover if I had something that money can't buy. As I explored this concept, I examined the effects that people had on one another. In most circumstances, as they interacted, I noticed that they walked away looking severely depleted. It was at that point that I made a vow to consider ways that my presence would leave people with a sense of fullness in their hearts, to the point of overflowing. What lasting impression are you leaving on people's hearts....life depleting or life giving?

## *Prayer*

*Lord, I thank You for the season in my life that prompted me to look deep within. Help me to continue to explore the commodity that lies within me that no amount of money can buy. I pray that with each encounter, I leave the person with a sense of life giving fullness. May it catch on like wildfire and create a never ending trend worldwide.*

# Personal Reflections

_____

_____

_____

_____

_____

_____

_____

_____

_____

_____

_____

_____

_____

# DAY 2

## Anger Management

*No temptation has overtaken you except what is common to mankind. And God is faithful; he will not let you be tempted beyond what you can bear. But when you are tempted, he will also provide a way out so that you can endure it.*

*– 1 Corinthians 10:13 (NIV)*

Are you struggling with an anger management problem? What would it take for you to be rid of this problem? Perhaps you think that you would not have an anger management problem if certain people would not provoke you to anger.

The truth of the matter is that while we are in this body there will be people and circumstances that provoke us to anger. We may be able to walk away from one person who gets under our skin but not too far down the path we will encounter another abrasive person. In order to have victory over an issue, God provides the training ground in order for us to have ample practice but at the same time He provides escape routes along the way so we will evade a full blown explosion. With that being said, everyone who provokes us to anger won't just miraculously disappear; it will require that we develop a strategy to check our anger meter along the way as we face annoyances.

Think for a minute about the engine in your car. If it runs low on coolant, it will overheat and eventually do some serious damage if it is not replenished. Likewise, our emotions are similar to car engines. When we lose our cool, even though it may seem like a spur of the moment occurrence, it is the furthest thing from the truth. Losing our cool is a process; thus, we can take precautionary measures by identifying the needed "coolant" and applying enough of it in order to refrain from getting overheated, especially when we know in advance that we will encounter certain stressors.

## *Prayer*

*Lord, I thank You that I am not alone in my struggles. I also thank you for the method of escape that You provide with every temptation I face so that I can experience victory over this anger issue.*

# Personal Reflections

_____

_____

_____

_____

_____

_____

_____

_____

_____

_____

_____

_____

_____

# DAY 3

# Two Less Lonely People

*Dear friends, let us love one another, for love comes from God. Everyone who loves has been born of God and knows God.*

*– 1 John 4:7 (NIV)*

On special occasions, my heart goes out to all the single people who are waiting on God to present to them Mr. or Mrs. Right. There is so much advertisement that goes into the promotion of gift exchange that it essentially alienates those who don't have a significant other with whom to share the occasion. At that time of year, many begin to question their self worth. They wonder if their life is of any value.

If this seems to be the story of your life, I'm here today to tell you that is a lie straight from the pit of hell. Your mere existence is of great wealth; you are worthy of being loved! Nevertheless, while you are in this season it is important to refrain from allowing your emotions to dictate your actions. In this time of singleness, refrain from doing something that you will later regret. Also, don't settle for less than what God has picked out for you for the mere purpose of evading being alone.

You have the power to combat loneliness on a personal level and at the same time make it a less lonely occasion for someone else. There is a song titled Two Less Lonely People in the World that speaks to this situation. Reach out to another lonely person with a brotherly or sisterly kind of love and you will be a participant in ensuring that there will be two less lonely people.

## *Prayer*

*Lord, I am thankful for relationships. Help me to be sensitive to those who appear to be lonely. Also, help me to take part in making their journey in life a less lonely experience.*

# Personal Reflections

_____

_____

_____

_____

_____

_____

_____

_____

_____

_____

_____

_____

_____

_____

# DAY 4

## Sealed With a Kiss

*Greet one another with a holy kiss.*
*–2 Corinthians 13:12 (NIV)*

Have you been kissed lately? There is something very special about a kiss. That is evident in fairy tales as well as real life. Take for instance the account of Snow White. Even though the story is based on a fairy tale, there is great truth behind the principle of her need for a warm embrace. Her lifeless body required a special touch in order to be awakened. She, like everyone else, was created for relationship. The warm touch of another human does amazing things to the body. It increases the heart rate, dilates the blood vessels and causes brain chemicals to be released.

Unbeknownst to you, you probably come in contact with people every day who are silently dreaming to be the recipient of a touch from another human being in order to awaken hope in their feeble souls. On the surface it may appear that they have everything together but on the inside they may be hanging on for dear life by a thin thread. As a matter of fact, you may be that person.

God has a strong desire to get His life-giving kisses from heaven to earth. He works through you and me to reach out and share a warm embrace with another. Even though a kiss may not be appropriate in all situations, there are so many other means of sharing God's life-giving kisses. Just to mention a few, you can share a smile, a kind word or perform a kind deed. These gestures are free and have an amazing impact. Would you join me today in being a vessel in sharing God's heavenly kisses with a world of hurting people?

## *Prayer*

*Lord, help me to not withhold the warm embrace that You would like to extend to everyone I come in contact with today.*

# Personal Reflections

_____

_____

_____

_____

_____

_____

_____

_____

_____

_____

_____

_____

_____

## Got Peace?

*If it is possible, as far as it depends on you, live at peace with everyone.*

*– Romans 12:18 (NIV)*

Have you lost your cool lately? Perhaps there is someone in your home, workplace, school or even in your church that annoys you to no end. Due to that person's words or actions, you may feel totally justified in telling them exactly what you think about them. Many times this is done in a less than tactful way.

Even though you feel that it is completely in order to give them a piece of your mind, it is important to remember that a knee jerk response may not be beneficial in the long run. If you care at all about the long term implications, it is definitely important that you pick your battles wisely. When you are in the heat of a disagreement, the focus typically is honed in on the issue at hand to the point that we forget to step back and readjust our lens to view it in light of life as a whole.

With the average life expectancy for men being 76 years of age, that equates to over 665,760 hours. With that being said, many of our disagreements occur over a matter of minutes and we forfeit so much because we fail to view the issue in light of the overall picture of life. Many of us have lost valuable relationships, employment and other things that we hold dear to our hearts because we don't count the cost of words spoken in haste.

## *Prayer*

*Lord, help me to pick my battles wisely and to be proactive in processing my potential response in light of how it will affect my life as a whole.*

# Personal Reflections

_____

_____

_____

_____

_____

_____

_____

_____

_____

_____

_____

_____

_____

_____

# DAY 6

## Out of Heart, Out of Mind

*The weapons we fight with are not the weapons of the world. On the contrary, they have divine power to demolish strongholds. We demolish arguments and every pretension that sets itself up against the knowledge of God, and we take captive every thought to make it obedient to Christ.*

*– 2 Corinthians 10:4-5 (NIV)*

Is there a certain person that you can't seem to get out of your thoughts? Perhaps it is someone who has wronged you in some way. Perhaps that person continues to wrong you and he or she doesn't even bother to apologize. Do you find yourself mulling over the details of the negative encounters with that person? Perhaps the emotional pain from the encounters has cut so deep that you don't think that you can bear it.

Have you ever wondered why you continue to allow those encounters to plague your mind? Perhaps you are not very assertive thus subconsciously you feel that if you build up enough resentment towards that person then you will be able to protect yourself from future attacks.

Better yet, perhaps you don't feel that justice is being done within your perceived acceptable timetable so you create scenarios in your mind of how you will pay back evil with evil.

Truth being told, if that person is not on your heart then he or she should not be in your head. Unless you are in a position whereas you are committed to pray for blessings and a God encounter over that person, he or she should not be present in your thoughts. Nevertheless, even though you may not be responsible for the things that happened to you, you are responsible for your response to those encounters.

## *Prayer*

*Lord, help me to take captive every thought that is contrary to Your Word. I forgive all those who have wronged me. I pray that You bless them and help them to come to know You in such a deep and personal way.*

# Personal Reflections

_____

_____

_____

_____

_____

_____

_____

_____

_____

_____

_____

_____

_____

# DAY 7

## The Beautiful Letdown

*And my God will meet all your needs according to the riches of his glory in Christ Jesus.*
*– Philippians 4:19 (NIV)*

How well do you know Jesus? As with any other relationship, it requires a certain level of vulnerability to create an intimate relationship. As we engage in relationships with other human beings we learn very quickly that they are very limited to what they can provide for the relationship. It is typically when the relationship is tried in certain areas that we discover what we can expect from that person.

We cannot expect one person to be our all in all. For instance, a friendship cannot provide certain things that a marriage can provide. With every relationship that is tried and fails our expectations in certain areas, it is an opportunity for us to see how Jesus is willing and able to fill in the gaps. As hard as it may be for us to experience letdowns in our relationships, it actually becomes a beautiful letdown.

Jesus would love to become our all in all. That is not a title that comes easy though. It is a title that comes through painful experiences, whereas others fail to be our all in all. The reason why they fail us in certain areas is because human beings were never meant to fill our every need. Only Jesus was preordained to be our all in all. He wants to be our primary source. He meets all of our spiritual needs and if it involves a physical need, He will either see to it that the need gets met or He will change our perspective to realize that it wasn't actually a need after all.

## *Prayer*

*Lord, I thank You for the times when aspects of my relationships didn't meet every one of my needs. It was times like those that pushed me closer to You and allowed me to see that only a perfect Savior could fill every need and become my all in all.*

# Personal Reflections

# DAY 8

# Easily Offended?

*Great peace have they which love thy law: and nothing shall offend them.*

*– Psalm 119:165 (KJV)*

Do you find yourself easily offended? Perhaps you see it as justified anger because someone said or did something to hurt you. After all, if you do not express your emotions toward the offender then you could potentially be viewed as a doormat, right? Also, if you let this offense go it could potentially make you desensitized to addressing future offenses.

Nevertheless, at the moment the offense is taken a transaction of ownership occurs within. Similar to a new born baby, the offense longs to be nursed shortly after being born. Thereafter, the offense craves to be nursed again and again until it virtually becomes a nonstop activity. As pressing things go unattended as the mom makes her newborn the main focal point of her attention, the same is so with the offense.

Don't be mistaken, it is not that you are called to ignore or suppress the offense. Instead, you should acknowledge to the Lord that the offense was painful and at the same time surrender that pain to Him. It is important to refrain from allowing the offense to have power over your thoughts or actions. Victory is won when the offense is stripped of its power and nailed to the cross to never be picked up again.

## *Prayer*

*Lord, I thank You for the amazing examples You set as You never internalized an offense but allowed it to be striped of its power as You were nailed to the cross. I thank You for taking it a step further by asking our Heavenly Father to forgive Your offenders. Help me to follow suit.*

# Personal Reflections

# DAY 9

## Come Up Higher

*And we all, who with unveiled faces contemplate the Lord's glory, are being transformed into his image with ever-increasing glory, which comes from the Lord, who is the Spirit.*

*— 2 Corinthians 3:18 (NIV)*

Has encouragement from another helped to shape the person you have become? There is just something extremely empowering about someone believing in you in a manner greater than you believe in yourself. You just can't help but rise to the occasion. It seems as though the encouragement takes someone who has been in a bent over state and instills in them the courage to rise up, stand tall and become all that they were created to become.

Essentially that is what Christ did for each one of us. He saw us in our bent over state as we were wasting away in sin. He poured His courage inside of us, all the while calling us to rise above to a higher moral standard of living. When He gazed upon us He did not see our current state but He saw who we would become once our total transformation from glory to glory reached completion.

We have the awesome opportunity to mimic Christ by encouraging others to be more than they could ever envision for themselves. Encouragement is so effective, hence the reason each team in the sports arena has their own cheering squad. Imagine what the world would be like if everyone had their own personal cheerleader.

## *Prayer*

*Lord, I thank You for looking past who I am and seeing who I will become. Help me to do the same for others by extending that same level of encouragement to help them come up higher.*

# Personal Reflections

_____

_____

_____

_____

_____

_____

_____

_____

_____

_____

_____

_____

_____

_____

## DAY 10

# Carry Each Other's Burdens

*Carry each other's burdens, and in this way you will fulfill the law of Christ.*
*– Galatians 6:2 (NIV)*

If we had the ability to view things through a spiritual lens, we would probably see one another nestled under a pile of burdens. Whether we recognize it or not, each time we request something of another person we essentially add a measure of weight to their pile of burdens. This is especially so around the holiday season. It seems that everyone has a longer "to do list" at that time of year.

In my attempt to make Christ known throughout the day, I ask God to show me ways that I can be of service to Him. One very practical impression He has placed on my heart is to set aside a little time each day to lighten someone else's burden. Simply being of service to help lighten the burden of another person, without asking for anything in return, has proved to have a huge impact.

One profound example of carrying another person's burden is depicted as Simon helped Jesus carry His cross on the road to face His crucifixion. As Jesus died on that cross, He set the paramount example of carrying the burden of another as the sins of the entire world was heaped upon His back. Even though no one will ever be called to repeat the work that only Jesus could accomplish, we do have the opportunity to help lighten the burden of another in practical ways.

## *Prayer*

*Lord, help me to carve out time in my busy schedule to be available to be used by You. Show me practical ways that I can help carry the burden of another in order for Your love to show forth through me.*

# Personal Reflections

# DAY 11

# Who's Who

*Nothing impure will ever enter it, nor will anyone who does what is shameful or deceitful, but only those whose names are written in the Lamb's book of life.*

*– Revelation 21:27 (NIV)*

There are so many prestigious list that people strive to be on. Among those lists are Forbes 500, Who's Who, Lifestyles of the Rich and Famous, the Dean's List, etc. The hope of making it on these lists is to get recognition and be viewed as "a somebody". Striving to be "a somebody" takes a lot of energy. It can be self consuming. One question remains; once the individual makes it to the top, then what?

There is nothing wrong, in and of itself, with being on one of these lists. It depends on where the focus rest in the process of getting there. If the focus is merely bent on prestige, then being on top can still prove to leave people feeling empty and all alone. That scenario is obvious as we look to society. People who seem to be on top of their game turn to drugs, alcohol and relationships for fulfillment or to numb the pain of dissatisfaction.

Having your name listed in the Lamb's Book of Life is the only list that can ever bring true contentment. There are so many things in life that are fleeting. This is the only list that is everlasting and will stand the test of time. Even if you are considered "a nobody" in this world your entire life, if your name appears on this list, you are looked upon by God as a prized possession. In God's eyes you, my friend, are "a somebody".

## *Prayer*

*Lord, I thank You that in Your eyes I am "a somebody". I relinquish my desire to compete with the world. If by chance my name makes it on one of these worldly list in the process of serving You, to You be all the glory and honor.*

# Personal Reflections

_____

_____

_____

_____

_____

_____

_____

_____

_____

_____

_____

_____

_____

_____

_____

_____

# DAY 12

## VIP Status

*The gatekeeper opens the gate for him, and the sheep listen to his voice. He calls his own sheep by name and leads them out.*
*– John 10:3 (NIV)*

Have you ever been stereotyped amongst a group of people based of your ethnicity, race or gender? Better yet, are you recognized by others based on your past? In that sense, the world can prove to be very unforgiving. Too often people get their identity from what they do or have done rather than from who they were created to become.

The human heart longs to be recognized as a one-of-a-kind unique individual. It also longs to be accepted right where it is...faults and all. It longs to be identified as the special creation that God has brought forth into existence. Think about how it makes you feel when you run into someone you just recently met and they address you by name. There is something so special about another person taking the time to know you on a personal level. It seems to awaken a sense of importance deep down on the inside.

Unlike humans, God has a whole universe of names to remember but yet He calls each of us by name. He doesn't have favorites or make a concerted effort to remember a person's name solely based on their social status or based on what that person can do for Him. He refrains from grouping us by our similarities but recognizes us and calls us by name based on our one-of-a-kind uniqueness.

## *Prayer*

*Lord, help me to refrain from stereotyping people but to treat each person based on their VIP status in You. Help me to mimic Your example by making an effort to remember and address each and every person by name, not only those who are capable of doing something to benefit me.*

# Personal Reflections

# DAY 13

## The Prodigal

*Not long after that, the younger son got together all he had, set off for a distant country and there squandered his wealth in wild living. When he came to his senses, he said, How many of my father's hired servants have food to spare, and here I am starving to death! I will set out and go back to my father and say to him: Father, I have sinned against heaven and against you. So he got up and went to his father. But while he was still a long way off, his father saw him and was filled with compassion for him; he ran to his son, threw his arms around him and kissed him.*

*– Luke 15:13; 17-18; 20 (NIV)*

Perhaps you have a friend or family member who is on the brink of self-destruction. Are you on standby for that certain someone to mess up so that you can give them a heaping dose of "I told you so?" Perhaps you feel that it is your God given calling to set that person straight. That is, since you have your life in perfect order and you have been afforded the opportunity to clearly see the error of their ways.

When we are eager to point out the error of someone's ways, we need to first check our motive. Are we wanting them to pay for their actions or are we eager to see them restored to the Father? Over and over in scripture, it is evident that the best lessons are not those that are taught but those that are caught. Self-discovery is such a powerful tool...there is great depth to the experiences that involve self-discovery. It is a realization that is derived after much travailing...in a sense, wrestling with God to get to this point.

The truth of the matter is that not one of us has our lives in perfect order. The only one who has His life in perfect order is Jesus. Nevertheless, even though He had His life in perfect order He was never puffed up with feelings of self-righteousness. Before you deal with the prodigal in your life, will you pause and take note of our Heavenly Father's perfect picture of how He dealt with people who have gone astray?

## *Prayer*

*Lord, I thank You for reminding me of my imperfections so that I can respond with love and mercy to those who have gone astray. I thank You for helping me to see that Your motive is not to inflict punishment on Your children but it is always to bring about restoration.*

## Personal Reflections

_____

_____

_____

_____

_____

_____

_____

_____

# DAY 14

# The Blame Game

*And he said, "Who told you that you were naked? Have you eaten from the tree that I commanded you not to eat from?" The man said, "The woman you put here with me — she gave me some fruit from the tree, and I ate it." Then the Lord God said to the woman, "What is this you have done?" The woman said, "The serpent deceived me, and I ate."*

*– Genesis 3:11-13 (NIV)*

Like Adam and Eve, do you find yourself playing the blame game when you sin? Do you look for a scapegoat to carry the weight of your sin? Let's think this through for a moment. If you are not to blame for your sin then what does that make you? That's right…that would make you a victim at the hands of another person's wrong doing. Once we unload our sin on a scapegoat, we fool ourselves into thinking that we can walk away free and clear of the offense. Nevertheless, when we play the victim role that is only the beginning of the offense.

Victimhood limits our perception of our power to change. It defines us by our experience and we stay stuck. It renders us as a powerless individual incapable of mustering up the strength to rise above. Also, evading the responsibility of taking ownership of our sin creates a separation between us and the Lord. Like Adam and Eve, we hide from Him in fear of being found out...as if He doesn't already know about the offense.

The only way to break free from the victim mentality is to make an about face turn away from the sin and to ask for forgiveness. Our life is like a timeline and the moment we ask for forgiveness it becomes an intersecting line that divides our past sin from the life we were predestined to live. The old sinful way is representative of Christ's death and the other side, whereas we are walking in freedom from the sin, is representative of His resurrection. Before Christ, we were enslaved to sin but with Christ, we receive velvet chains of righteousness holding us securely next to the chest of our Father.

## *Prayer*

*Lord, I realize that when I play the blame game it shows that I am expressing a lack of love for You and the person I am attempting to blame for the error of my ways. I take ownership for my choice to sin and I ask for forgiveness from sinning against You and that person.*

# Personal Reflections

# DAY 15

# Letting Go of the Past

*The Spirit of the Sovereign Lord is on me, because the Lord has anointed me to proclaim good news to the poor. He has sent me to bind up the brokenhearted, to proclaim freedom for the captives and release from darkness for the prisoners, to proclaim the year of the Lord's favor and the day of vengeance of our God, to comfort all who mourn, and provide for those who grieve in Zion—to bestow on them a crown of beauty instead of ashes, the oil of joy instead of mourning, and a garment of praise instead of a spirit of despair. They will be called oaks of righteousness, a planting of the Lord for the display of his splendor.*
*– Isaiah 61:1-3 (NIV)*

Have you ever ventured off into a danger zone, all the while unaware that danger was lurking around the corner? Perhaps there was so much external and internal turmoil that you were shielded from being able to think logically. Even still, perhaps you saw the warning signs but felt a bit invincible so you blatantly ignored them.

Even though the Bible clearly warns us about the danger of harping on the past, many times we ignore those instructions and decide to venture off into the danger zone. Even though it may not have been our original intent, we tend to set up camp there. For some unknown reason, we feel that if we nurse, curse or rehearse the painful memories from the past it will somehow make the pain go away. Contrary to that, reliving the past does just the opposite. It confines us to a holding cell of torment in the brain. Hence, everything and everyone advances forward except for us.

Nevertheless, God wants so much more for us in reference to our experience here on this earth. It's not that He is not interested in hearing about our painful past; He just does not want us to become a prisoner to that experience. If we release the painful memories into His capable hands, He has a supernatural way of reversing the negative effects of the deep-rooted wounds. If you surrender your past to Him you will not be disappointed… He is sure to give you beauty in return for your ashes.

## *Prayer*

Lord, I thank You that You desire for me to be set free from past hurts and live an abundant life. I realize that I can't start a new chapter in my life if I keep re-reading the last one. I vow to no longer allow my painful past to dictate my future.

## Personal Reflections

_____

_____

_____

_____

_____

_____

_____

# DAY 16

## Proactive Parenting

*Train up a child in the way he should go [and in keeping with his individual gift or bent], and when he is old he will not depart from it.*
— *Proverbs 22:6 (AMP)*

**A**t times, do you feel that you would love to have the carefree spirit of a child? They seem to enjoy life to the fullest. It seems that even their teachable moments are done in a manner that is centered on fun. The entertainment element helps to engage them and make them more apt to retain the information. It is typically exciting for them since they are not under the constraints of rigid guidelines. Nevertheless, scripture shows that rest from the mundane routine is purposeful, even God rested on the Sabbath.

On the flip side, even though at times we would like for life to solely be about the entertainment element, through God's actions, we can see that the daily routine is also purposeful. Even God had a daily routine the remainder of the week. He subjected himself to self-imposed guidelines before He allowed Himself the day of rest. As parents, we must impart the importance of this balance to our children. Rarely will you find a child who is so self-disciplined that he or she doesn't need a parent to set healthy guidelines in reference to work and play. Similar to all other humans who bear a sin nature, kids typically have a bent toward doing only what will gratify the flesh.

Nevertheless, if parents are not proactive in setting specific guidelines then the parents essentially become reactive participants in the relationship. All too often we as parents allow our children too much free reign over their time and decisions. With that being said, the inevitable occurs when expectations are not clearly stated and enforced…the child eventually makes a poor decision that could prove to be quite costly. Unfortunately, this leads the parent in a tailspin of having to use the infamous word "don't" on a repetitive basis. It basically sets the child up for failure and takes more energy and effort on the parent's part. Will you join me in loving our children enough to teach and enforce Godly principles in reference to work and play so that they will rise to the occasion and take hold of God's unique purpose and plan for their lives?

# *Prayer*

Lord, I thank You for my children's carefree spirit. At the same time, please help me to refrain from promoting too much freedom to the detriment of breaching healthy boundaries and guidelines that they so desperately need. Give me wisdom, knowledge and understanding in order to keep them hemmed in, protected from all that stems from idleness and prepped for success in order to carry out their divine God-given assignment.

## Personal Reflections

_____

_____

_____

_____

_____

_____

_____

# DAY 17

## Givers Gain

*Give, and it will be given to you. A good measure, pressed down, shaken together and running over, will be poured into your lap. For with the measure you use, it will be measured to you.*

*– Luke 6:38 (NIV)*

**W**ho is in your circle of influence? Better yet, who would you like to have in your inner circle? There are those who at just the mention of their names, others stand at attention. They find it a privilege to have it said that they are in some way connected to that person. Many go out of their way to assist these noteworthy people, all the while hoping that they will one day benefit from that connection.

Even though we were hardwired for relationship, it is important that we check the motive behind our desire to be connected to others. Our desire should not be focused on what that person can do for us. Instead, it should be focused on how we can make that person's life richer. If you commit to the relationship over the long haul, you will see that givers always gain.

There is one name that carries an enormous amount of influence. Since the beginning of time, there is no other name that has consistently had the impact like the name of Jesus. Even still, we should not seek a relationship with Him for the fringe benefits. Nevertheless, as we press in and invest in the relationship, all the while submitting to His desire for our lives, we will automatically gain far more than we could ever give.

## *Prayer*

*Lord, thank You so much for Your Son setting the ultimate example as He gave His life as a ransom so that we all could gain eternal life. Please open my spiritual eyes to see those who are in desperate need of hearing how they can give their lives to Jesus so that they can gain this ultimate gift.*

# Personal Reflections

# DAY 18

# Filtered Speech

*"Woe to me!" I cried. "I am ruined! For I am a man of unclean lips, and I live among a people of unclean lips, and my eyes have seen the King, the Lord Almighty."*

*– Isaiah 6:5 (NIV)*

Have you ever wondered what God would say about your speech if you met Him face to face today? Do you allow your speech to control you or do you have mastery over your mouth? Would others say that you are known for thinking before you speak or would they say that you are very loose with your words? Do you respond like the person who wants to express his opinion regardless of the cost thus adds the disclaimer, "well, I'm just saying"; as if that neutralizes the crudeness.

Even though you might not be constantly cognizant of the fact that God is eternally present, it does not change the fact that He is aware of everything that you say. He is also aware of the motive in your heart behind your speech. Unless God is prompting the response, there are some things that are better left unsaid. You may feel better at the moment as you air your emotions, but if your words were hurtful by any means, that feeling simply represents a false sense of satisfaction. Stating exactly what is on your mind without allowing your words to be filtered by the Holy Spirit typically makes matters worse in the long run.

Praying about a situation before speaking is one of the wisest things you can do. Grant it, it may not yield immediate results or give you the instant gratification that you seek. Nevertheless, silence in certain situations is golden. As you allow God to initiate a change within an individual, it is sure to yield positive results. God's method changes the person from the inside out; it bypasses a behavioral adjustment and goes deep beneath the surface to make a heart adjustment.

## *Prayer*

*Lord, I bring my thought life before You so that You can weed through the things that do not need to manifest into words. May my speech be life giving as opposed to causing damage to my relationships.*

# Personal Reflections

# DAY 19

## Cost vs Benefits

*Then Jesus said to his disciples, "Whoever wants to be my disciple must deny themselves and take up their cross and follow me".*
*– Matthew 16:24 (NIV)*

**W**ould you agree that there is a cost to following Jesus? Depending on where you live or the state of your current situation, the cost to you may be higher than that of others. Nevertheless, there is always a cost. With that cost there is a choice that each one of us has to make as to whether we are willing to pay the price.

Even the mere act of carving out quiet time to spend with Him will require that you sacrifice time spent elsewhere. Following Him may also require that you forfeit relationships that are no longer conducive to living a righteous life. No matter how spiritually unhealthy a relationship may be, it's not always easy to simply walk away. Regardless, an intimate relationship with Him is far more gratifying than any unwholesome relationship.

You may wonder why a relationship with Him is so costly. The truth of the matter is that our sin has cost this man His life. The cost that we pay is minuscule in comparison to the price He paid in order to restore the severed connection between heaven and earth. The benefits, on the other hand, far outweigh the cost. As we carve out time to spend with Him, He supernaturally empowers us to maximize our time and streamline our efforts to the point where we can get more done in less time. In addition to supernatural time management, the peace in our hearts derived from a relationship with Him is priceless.

## *Prayer*

*Lord, I thank You that You set the ultimate example of following the perfect will of the Father. I thank You that the fringe benefits of following You far outweigh the cost.*

# Personal Reflections

# DAY 20

## Conflict Resolution

*What causes fights and quarrels among you? Don't they come from your desires that battle within you? You desire but do not have, so you kill. You covet but you cannot get what you want, so you quarrel and fight. You do not have because you do not ask God. When you ask, you do not receive, because you ask with wrong motives, that you may spend what you get on your pleasures. Submit yourselves, then, to God. Resist the devil, and he will flee from you.*

*– James 4:1-3, 7 (NIV)*

Have you been involved in a disagreement recently? What was the outcome? Do you even remember the initial reason for the disagreement or were you so bent on winning the argument that you lost track of it? Did you focus solely on the issue that was being discussed or did you feel the need to unload the ammunition comprised of that person's past shortcomings as well?

It is important to remember that the opinions of both parties are valued in a healthy relationship. Love says, "Your opinions and desires matter." No one person should constantly feel the need to be the victor in the face of disagreements. To the contrary, that person ends up losing in the end because a little something tends to die in that relationship every time the other party is devalued. A relationship worth having requires compromise… anything else does not constitute a relationship. The one who lacks a desire for compromise would be better off narrowing his circle of influence to me, myself and I…in that way, he would be assured of a favorable outcome.

Any time there is a disagreement, it necessitates that we first examine our motives. Disagreements do not need to be viewed as something to be avoided at all cost. It simply means that the two people were not created exactly alike and are merely embracing their individuality. The problem arises when the two people do not possess healthy conflict resolution skills. Primarily, the resolution needs to be God centered as opposed to being me centered. The focus should rest on what will bring about the most glory to God? Relationships were ordained by God thus we should value the other person as a highly favored child of God.

## *Prayer*

*Lord, I thank You for blessing me with relationships. Help me to respect and honor the opinions and desires of others in a way that brings You the utmost glory.*

## Personal Reflections

_____

_____

_____

_____

_____

_____

_____

_____

# DAY 21

# Which Came First, the Chicken or the Egg?

*If it is possible, as far as it depends on you, live at peace with everyone.*
*– Romans 12:18 (NIV)*

Have you ever wondered which came first, the chicken or the egg? This scenario is also known as the granddaddy of causality dilemmas. It is geared toward one's ability to reach into a constant circular cycle and be able to determine which serves as the cause and which serves as the consequence. With that being said, you must take into consideration that X is not possible to exist without the presence of Y and Y is not able to exist without the presence of X.

The question about the chicken and the egg is probably based on a concept centered on evolution. Nevertheless, for those of us who trust the Word as being inerrant, the answer is short and sweet...the chicken came first, of course. This conclusion stems from the first chapter of Genesis whereas God created all the living creatures of the sky, water and ground then He gave them the instruction to be fruitful and multiply.

As one tries to determine who is to blame in a troubled relationship, it is not as clear cut as the chicken and egg scenario. The constant circular cycle of chaotic activity with random shots being fired from both sides makes it extremely difficult to reach in and accurately pinpoint the cause and consequence. If you find yourself amidst such turmoil, the key element should not be based on figuring out who is to blame as it should be based on choosing to be an active participant in breaking the dysfunctional cycle. It is time to recommit to living a proactive life based on the call to action from God as opposed to reacting based on circumstances and emotions.

## *Prayer*

*Lord, thank You for revealing to me that in the grand scheme of things, it is not important that I win the blame game. I trust that as I fix my eyes on You and respond in a proactive manner based on the principles set forth in Your Word, it will essentially set me up for success and give me ample room to deal with unexpected difficulties.*

# Personal Reflections

_____

_____

_____

_____

_____

_____

_____

_____

_____

_____

_____

_____

_____

_____

# DAY 22

## Blind Love

*Above all, love each other deeply, because love covers over a multitude of sins.*
*— 1 Peter 4:8 (NIV)*

Have you ever heard someone say, "I don't know how you can possibly be in a relationship with that person?" (In this scenario, the reference is not made about people who are abusive but about those who have idiosyncrasies that make others annoyed). It is true that people can be really difficult to get along with at times. This is especially so when we hone in on our differences and view those differences in a negative sense.

Having only one person who is able to tolerate our idiosyncrasies on a long term basis can prove to be very positive. If that were not the case then we would not value our current relationship but instead we would be more apt to go from relationship to relationship. In a sense, this blind love keeps invisible boundaries lines around us.

Nevertheless, if a couple has prayerfully sought God's direction before becoming one then they can be certain that God will provide them with the grace needed in order to deal with their differences. After all, He knew of their differences beforehand. God's foreknowledge of this is evident in Psalm 139:16. It states, "Your eyes saw my unformed body; all the days ordained for me were written in Your book before one of them came to be." Thus, when God designed each person in his or her mother's womb, He not only designed them to fit His purpose and plan for existence but their intricate design was custom made to be compatible with their spouse.

## *Prayer*

*Lord, thank You for the time and attention You took to form each individual so that they can be compatible with one very special and specific person. Help us to respect and celebrate our differences.*

# Personal Reflections

_____

_____

_____

_____

_____

_____

_____

_____

_____

_____

_____

_____

_____

# DAY 23

# Arranged Marriage

*Marry and have sons and daughters; find wives for your sons and give your daughters in marriage, so that they too may have sons and daughters. Increase in number there; do not decrease.*

*– Jeremiah 29:6 (NIV)*

**A**re you single? How do you feel about an arranged marriage? In the Old Testament, the father would choose a spouse for his sons and daughters. This was done because he was seen as the shepherd of the family. As the shepherd, his job was to watch over his flock and protect them from predators that did not have their best interest at heart.

Do you feel comfortable enough to allow someone to choose the mate they think would be best suitable for you? The one who is responsible for selecting the mate must have inside information about both parties. The problem rests in the fact that even though our earthly father may have extensive information about his own child, he probably only has limited information about the prospective mate. He may do a great job at selecting the mate but there is someone else who has a perfect tract record in this department.

Although an earthly father has some limitations from his vantage point, our Heavenly Father does not. When He looks at his children, He sees a snapshot from our pre-birth state all the way through to our eternal state in heaven. God will not choose solely based on our current circumstances. He factors in our past disappointments, hurts, victories, strengths and weaknesses. He is trustworthy because He never has a hidden agenda and only wants the very best for us.

# *Prayer*

*Lord, I pray that all singles will surrender to You to select their mates. You are the only one who is capable of making an infallible selection.*

# Personal Reflections

# DAY 24

## Are You Commited?

*God is not human, that he should lie, not a human being, that he should change his mind. Does he speak and then not act? Does he promise and not fulfill?*

*– Numbers 23:19 (NIV)*

Who or what are you committed to? Commitment is a word that has lost the intensity of its meaning. A commitment used to be bound by a verbal agreement and a hand shake. In the here and now, for many of us, it requires written contracts and a legal system to get us to stay true to our commitments. Even still, when we no longer want to abide by the commitment we try to prove that it was faulty from the onset.

According to the Bible, when God made a promise it was a binding and everlasting commitment. By God's example we are able to see that a commitment is not based on emotions that are subject to change. A commitment is based on a predetermined decision to stick with something regardless of external circumstances.

The word commitment is defined as the act of engaging oneself. Yielding just a part of yourself will not give you the desired outcome; it involves a commitment of your whole being. The commitment should also involve a third party. That third party participant should be the Lord. Thus, when circumstances make it hard to stay true to the commitment, it becomes possible if we adhere to it as though we are doing it unto the Lord.

## *Prayer*

*Lord, today I commit to staying true to my commitments by bringing my mind, body and soul under the submission of Your Lordship.*

# Personal Reflections

# DAY 25

## Are You a Thermometer or a Thermostat?

*Therefore, if your whole body is full of light, and no part of it dark, it will be just as full of light as when a lamp shines its light on you.*
*– Luke 11:36 (NIV)*

**D**o you have the ability to detect the temperature of the atmosphere when you walk into a room? I am not speaking about whether it is hot or cold but in reference to the spiritual temperature. One obvious way to detect the spiritual temperature is by examining people's attitudes and emotional expressions.

If you have lived long enough, you will know that being a human thermometer doesn't involve rocket science. Most of us do this without much thought each time we walk into any given environment. For example, if you walk into a room where two people have just engaged in an argument it is not necessary for them to tell you what just happened. It is typically obvious even if no words are spoken. Figuratively speaking, the tension is so thick you could cut it with a knife. There is a negative overtone that lingers in the air due to the emotional stress and strain.

One thing that is quite challenging is to take being a human thermometer one step further by becoming a human thermostat. The instant a thermostat detects that the temperature is not adequate; it makes a shift to correct the temperature. From a humanistic standpoint, it requires a great deal of quiet time with the Lord to become a human thermostat. We must get to the point where we are empty of self and filled with the Spirit in order to bring about a positive shift in the atmosphere. If not, we too may fall prey to that same negative spirit. The positive shift will usher in the light and brighten even the darkest situations.

## *Prayer*

*Lord, help me to spend an adequate amount of time with you in order to get to a point that I am rid of self and completely filled with Your Spirit. As I allow Your Spirit to take over, I know it will bring about a positive shift in any negative environment I encounter.*

# Personal Reflections

_____

_____

_____

_____

_____

_____

_____

_____

_____

_____

_____

_____

_____

_____

# DAY 26

## Are Relationships Purposeful?

*I have given them the glory that you gave me, that they may be one as we are one — I in them and you in me — so that they may be brought to complete unity. Then the world will know that you sent me and have loved them even as you have loved me.*

*— John 17:22-23 (NIV)*

**D**o you have a social networking account? Once you create an account, it won't be long before you will realize that there is an underlying competition to see how many friends one can accumulate on the site. Unfortunately, there are those who fail to use a filtration system when getting a friend request because their main focus is adding to their numbers.

At times we can become so focused on the number of friends we have, to the point that we gravitate toward the vast majority of acquaintances who simply tolerate us rather than building deep lasting relationships with those who celebrate us. Many people don't recognize that there is a reason behind their desire for relationship.

It is woven into the very fabric of our beings. It dates back to eternity past. God and Jesus were one thus we were created for oneness...oneness with the Father and the Son and oneness with each other.

The problem arises when we confuse God's purpose for relationship with man's limited understanding of his basic need for connection. Relationships were not created for the sole purpose of our pleasure, but for God's glory. Relationships that we experience on this earth were designed to mimic the connection that the Father has with the Son. Hence, a key purpose for our connection with each other is so that our Christ-like interaction will be a witness to the world and draw them closer to Him.

## *Prayer*

*Lord, help me to remember that relationships were not created as a status symbol to boost my ego nor to gratify my flesh but to be used as a testimony to the world about the significance of oneness. Help me to hold in high esteem that which unifies me with other believers.*

# Personal Reflections

# DAY 27

## Addicted to Compliments?

*So God created mankind in his own image, in the image of God he created them; male and female he created them. God saw all that he had made, and it was very good. And there was evening, and there was morning—the sixth day.*

*— Genesis 1:27, 31 (NIV)*

**W**hen was the last time someone paid you a compliment? What was your response? Did you receive it with gratitude? Did you wonder if their comment was backed by an ulterior motive? Instead of receiving the compliment with a simple thank you, did you have a negative response about yourself that basically cancelled out the compliment?

Many of us are addicted to compliments. It governs the way we act, the way we speak and especially the way we dress. We become chameleons in the midst of those we are trying to impress. We long for the approval of others in regards to our performance and appearance. With all that being said, I think it is safe to say that mankind is definitely peculiar at times. Despite the fact that we long for approval, when someone pays us a compliment, we tend to down play it.

The reason so many of us are addicted to compliments is because we are discontent with various aspects of our being, whether it be our appearance, our talents or the lack thereof, or a certain aspect of our personality, etc. Despite the way we feel about ourselves, God thinks the world of us. It is the only time during His creation process that He declared His work to be very good. Complaining about something that God has already declared to be very good is basically an insult to God's creative work.

## *Prayer*

*Lord, I thank You for making me, me. I repent for making negative comments about myself and feeling the need to be elevated by others in order to compensate for that discontentment. I am committed to changing the things that I can and graciously accepting and cherishing the things about myself that are simply part of Your design.*

# Personal Reflections

_____

_____

_____

_____

_____

_____

_____

_____

_____

_____

_____

_____

_____

_____

_____

# DAY 28

# Think Before You Speak

*And whatever you do, whether in word or deed, do it all in the name of the Lord Jesus, giving thanks to God the Father through him.*
*– Colossians 3:17 (NIV)*

**D**o you think before you speak? What is the motive behind your words? If people take too long to reply in conversation, do you find yourself completing their sentences as well? Does your body language convey a message? Typically our body language speaks louder than words. After all, we live in such a fast paced world that our body language conveys the message that our time is too precious to waste on moments of silence.

The truth of the matter is that if we would take time to really contemplate what needs to be said before releasing the words into the atmosphere, it would save us and others a great deal of time and heartache. We would not have to spend so much time trying to undo so many hurtful words. It is said that it takes approximately five positive words to negate one negative word. That, my friend, appears to be a time waster in itself.

Thank goodness God knew in advance that we would struggle with this issue, thus He left written instruction to help us overcome negative speech. We are told that all of our words should be spoken in the name of Jesus. As we sift our words through His filtration system, it affords us the opportunity to discern the difference between the words that would not meet His standards from those that would bring glory to His name.

## *Prayer*

*Lord, thank You for Jesus who resides in me and serves as my internal filtration system to weed out unwholesome words. I commit to giving more thought to my choice of words before I speak and to allow others the same opportunity.*

# Personal Reflections

_____

_____

_____

_____

_____

_____

_____

_____

_____

_____

_____

_____

_____

_____

# DAY 29

# Overbooked?

*In all thy ways acknowledge him, and he shall direct thy paths.*

*– Proverbs 3:6 (KJV)*

**D**o you feel overwhelmed with your endless to do list? Perhaps you have more appointments than you do time. Perhaps several people have superimposed their own agenda onto your schedule. Unfortunately, because it is important to them they feel that it should be important to you.

The truth of the matter is that everyone has needs that must be fulfilled and just because it is a calling for one person does not mean that it is a calling for anyone and everyone. At times we even pull the guilt, desperation or greater than thou card to force people to get on board.

When we do this, we discount God's ability to speak to that person's heart to solicit involvement as He deems necessary.

In actuality, we should take our marching orders from the Lord himself. It is also important that we are sensitive to other people's schedules. We are all under God's umbrella and if we are sensitive to His voice as opposed to the demands that others impress upon us or that we impress upon others, we can be assured that He will not double book or overbook our schedules.

## *Prayer*

*Lord, I thank You that the calling You place on each person's life is of equal importance. Help me to not superimpose what I consider to be important onto someone else's schedule and help me to hold my ground when others are not respectful of my time.*

# Personal Reflections

---

---

---

---

---

---

---

---

---

---

---

---

---

---

# DAY 30

## Gifted

*Every good and perfect gift is from above, coming down from the Father of the heavenly lights, who does not change like shifting shadows.*

*– James 1:17 (NIV)*

**A**re you gifted in a particular area of your life? Perhaps you have recognized that you are gifted in more than one area. How do you use those gifts in relation to other people? Better yet, if those around you were polled in regards to the way you use your gifts, how do you think they would respond? Would they say that you get annoyed when you are asked to use your gifts to help others? Would they say that you use them as a tool to elevate yourself and belittle others? Or, would they say that you use them generously in a way that glorifies God?

Probably one of the most important aspects of the gift is to know from where it originated. Everything else seems to stem from that truth. The gifts do not originate from within as if we are the source of the giftedness...the gifts originate from above. Just as the gifts come from God they are to be used for God. Once we have a clear understanding and acceptance of that concept, then we will realize that the gifts are not ours to withhold.

As a matter of fact, we should be excited when we are asked to use our gifts. Our gifts are what make us unique and set us apart from the rest of society. If everyone possessed the same gift then there would only be a need for one of us. Our unique gifts give us our purpose for existence...we have an assignment here on this earth that has been tailor made for us in which no one else can accomplish.

## *Prayer*

*Lord, I thank You for knitting into my DNA gifts from above. As you place people in my path, I commit to using the gifts to bless them as a way to give back to You what You have so freely given to me.*

# Personal Reflections

_____

_____

_____

_____

_____

_____

_____

_____

_____

_____

_____

_____

_____

*"God will show Himself extraordinary as the ordinary yield to Him in service!"*

*— Leah Gonzales*

*In this inspiring daily devotional, Transcripts for Daily Living, Relationship Edition, Leah Gonzales expresses her passion to serve as an instrument to point others to the King of kings and the Lord of lords. These writings stem from her meditative time with Him; He takes her ordinary thoughts and creates an extraordinary message to share with others. As you too yield yourself to Him in service, He will add the "extra" to your ordinary.*

9214581R00074

Made in the USA
San Bernardino, CA
07 March 2014